It Could Still Be Water

By Allan Fowler

Consultants:
Robert L. Hillerich, Ph.D., Bowling Green
State University, Bowling Green, Ohio

Mary Nalbandian, Director of Science,
Chicago Public Schools, Chicago, Illinois

Fay Robinson, Child Development Specialist

CHILDRENS PRESS ®

CHICAGO

Design by Beth Herman Design Associates

Library of Congress Cataloging-in-Publication Data

Fowler, Allan
    It could still be water / by Allan Fowler.
      p. cm. –(Rookie read-about science)
      Summary: A simple description of the uses, properties,
  and forms of water
      ISBN 0-516-06003-1
      1. Water–Juvenile literature. [1. Water.] I. Title.
    II. Series: Fowler, Allan. Rookie read-about science.
GB662.3.F68 1992
553.7–dc20   92-7402
                                                                  CIP
                                                                  AC

Water! When you're thirsty,
you drink it.

When you're dirty, you
wash with it.

When you want to have
fun on a hot day, you swim
in it...

or sail on it in a boat.

You do so many things with water.

In fact, you couldn't live without water.

People, other animals, and plants...all must have water to live.

9

Most of the world is covered by water.

If you look at a globe,
you will see that the Earth
has much more water than
land.

Even your own body is
mostly water!

Water is a liquid. It's wet and you can pour it.

But water isn't always
a liquid.

Water could freeze until it becomes solid — and still be water.

An ice cube is a piece
of frozen water.

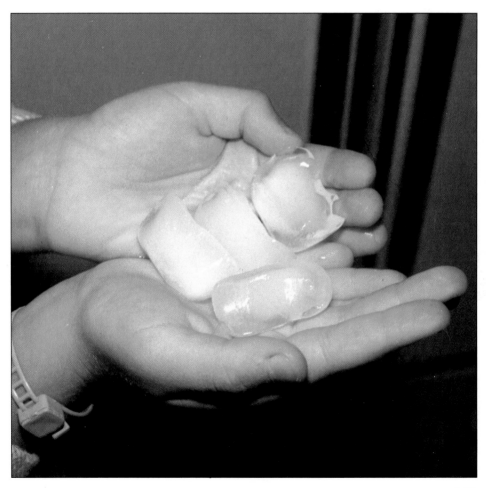

Water could rise into the air as tiny droplets called vapor and still be water.

Water vapor is invisible. You can't see it.

But if water vapor cools just enough, sometimes you can see it.

It could be the steam
coming out of a kettle...

or the vapor in your breath turning to mist on a very cold day...and still be water.

It could be thick fog you
can't see through...

or the clouds in the sky...
and still be water.

As the water droplets
in clouds cool, they get
bigger and bigger.

When they are cool enough, they fall to the ground as rain...

or freeze into snow.

27

So whether it's a funny
snowman...

or a fluffy cloud...
or a fish's home...
it could still be water!

Words You Know

water

liquid

solid

vapor

ice

clouds

fog

snow

rain

Earth

31

Index

About the Author

Allan Fowler is a free-lance writer with a background in advertising. Born in New York, he lives in Chicago now and enjoys traveling.

Photo Credits

NASA – 31 (bottom right)

PhotoEdit – ©Anna Zuckerman, Cover; ©Alan Oddie, 3, 4; ©Myrleen Ferguson, 5, 26; ©Richard Hutchings, 11; ©David Young-Wolff, 13; ©Jack S. Grove, 16, 30 (top center); ©Deborah Davis, 25, 31 (bottom left)

SuperStock International, Inc. – ©Beermann Collection, 10, 30 (top left)

Valan – ©Pierre Kohler, 6; ©Esther Schmidt, 8, 22, 31 (top left); ©Stephen J. Krasemann, 9; ©Dr. A. Farquhar, 12; ©Wayne Lankinen, 14, 30 (bottom left); ©V. Wilkinson, 17, 20, 21; ©Y. R. Tymstra, 19, 30 (top right); ©Ian Davis-Young, 23, 30 (bottom right); ©Tom W. Parkin, 24; ©Dennis W. Schmidt, 27, 31 (top right); ©Kennon Cooke, 28; ©R. Berchin, 29

COVER: Iceberg in water